Library of Congress Catalog Card Number 76–91871

ISBN 0 7232 1267 8

Printed in Great Britain by Cox & Wyman Ltd, Fakenham

'If you've got a load to move – get a Scammell.' This Scammell slogan sums up in a few words the purpose of this famous British company. Scammell Lorries Ltd of Watford, Hertfordshire, are very much 'specialist vehicle builders', i.e. specialist builders of specialist vehicles, and the name has come to be synonymous with 'big', 'sturdy' and 'indestructible'.

Looking back over the last 50 years, as we have done in this book, we find that many Scammells were tailor-made to meet the customer's particular requirements, incorporating, of course, as many contemporary standardised components as possible and practical. The early models could not always be described as handsome, but often this unintentional ugliness was an asset because it added to the impression of the vehicle's functional ability. And the function really was impressive! To present a complete pictorial history of Scammell vehicles is an impossible task because of their enormous variety and diversity. We have endeavoured, however, to illustrate the basic models and some of their derivations, including the military vehicles which played such an important role in World War II.

Our sincere thanks are extended to Scammell's enthusiastic Publicity Officers, past and present, for providing so many photographs for use in this book which of necessity has had to be restricted to about a tenth of its potential size. Much-appreciated assistance has also been rendered by Mr John Wynn, Director of Robert Wynn & Sons Ltd, and Mr E. G. Milne of Pickfords, two well-known heavy haulage specialists.

Piet Olyslager MSIA, MSAE, KIVI

The changing faces of Scammell, 1920–1970.

Large-scale motorisation of road transport started in earnest during the first World War, when thousands of load carriers were built for military purposes. After cessation of hostilities many ex-Service drivers joined the ranks of the road hauliers, using ex-WD vehicles of such famous makes as Albion, Commer, Dennis, FWD, Leyland, Packard and Peerless to name only a few. It was soon found that these vehicles could pull more than they could (or were supposed to) carry and firms like Carrimore offered semi-trailer conversions for the popular makes. These so-called 'articulated six-wheelers' provided an increase to about double the original payload rating. Although 'artics' were not a new invention they became quite popular during the early 1920s.

The legal status of such vehicles in Britain at this time had not been defined. There were no regulations in any Act of Parliament dealing with motor vehicles either for it or against it. Yet the advantages of the six-wheeled combination were obvious. Road Authorities complained about maximum legal axle weights and the six-wheeler more than met the objections because, although it was able to carry a heavier load than the four-wheeler, the maximum laden weight on any one axle was not more than six tons so the maximum legal weight of the total was not exceeded.

The firm of G. Scammell and Nephew Ltd recognised the advantages of such a vehicle and after consulting the appropriate authorities found that they would be within all legal requirements in producing it. The vehicle could be registered not as a truck with trailer but as one outfit and as the maximum axle weight did not exceed six tons its legal speed limit was 12 mph. It was also found that since the unladen (kerb) weight of the unit vehicle was less than five tons it was permitted to tow a six-ton trailer and that therefore a total payload of 13½-tons was legally permissible.

The first Scammell 'Artic' was designed during 1919 and in February 1920 the prototype vehicle made its first trial runs, taking just under 8 tons up West Hill in Highgate, London, in second gear. With the same load it achieved 18 mph on the level, and it took Swain's Lane in Hampstead after dropping to first gear but showing a useful margin of reserve power. Both hills, incidentally, were well known as testing places for heavy vehicles in London. Perhaps more important than the ability to climb these steep inclines, however, was the possibility of using the tractor in conjunction with two or more semi-trailers.

The name Scammell had been known from the early days of Queen Victoria's reign as a firm building carts and vans, and as wheelwrights, the founder being George Scammell. In 1913 the title of the firm became G. Scammell and Nephew Ltd. The nephew was the father of the late Lt.-Col. Alfred George Scammell D.S.O. The company had redeveloped a slum area in Fashion Street, Spitalfields, London E.1, and were well known as agents and official repairers for Foden Steam Wagons and Commer trucks (then called Commercars).

In 1921/22 a new factory was built in Watford, Herts., for the production of the new vehicle.

4A

4A: One of the earliest Scammells on a bridge somewhere in Persia.
5A: Pre-Watford Scammell 'Articulated Six-Wheeler' on show with a scale model and other sales aids. '7½ Tons at 3 Ton Cost and Speed'.
5B: The 4-cyl. 47.5-bhp engine had overhead valves.
5C: General view of bare chassis. Note separate suspension of turntable on tractor rear axle.
5D: Early swan-neck low-loader with winch, operated by the Post Office's Stores Dept.

5B

5A

5C

5D

In design the Scammell was not unlike the American Knox which had proved itself during the Great War as a tank transporter tractor in France and which was used in Britain by concerns such as Pickfords. The Knox featured an interesting turntable or 'fifth wheel' arrangement, whereby the turntable was mounted on heavy semi-elliptic springs attached directly to the rear axle of the tractor, while the weight of the tractor itself was carried on comparatively light underslung springs. Thus, the weight of the front end of the semi-trailer was carried, via the turntable, by the tractor's rear wheels without disturbing the tractor frame. The same design was used for the Scammell. In order to connect the semi-trailer to the turntable a single 'shoe' was provided which was locked by a spring trigger movement on the outside of the semi-trailer frame. By withdrawing the jaw the trailer could easily be detached from the tractor. The trailer's brakes were operated by the handbrake via a rod and bell crank arrangement in the centre of the turntable assembly.

The engine was a Scammell-built overhead valve unit with a maximum power output of 47.5 bhp at 1000 rpm. The four cylinders were cast in pairs and like the removable heads were made of 'aero engine iron'. Bore and stroke were 5 in. by 5½ in., giving a cubic capacity of just over 7 litres. The joints between cylinders and heads were made with two copper rings, and water was not passed between cylinder blocks and heads but by detachable exterior transfer ports.

The three-speed gearbox had a one-piece aluminium casing, carried, with the engine, in a subframe with three-point suspension. The gear shift 'gate' or striking gear was mounted on the gearbox. The clutch was of the Ferodo-faced internal cone type and connected to the gearbox by a universally jointed shaft. A second shaft took the drive from the gearbox to the bevel-driven differential gear of the counter- or jack-shaft from where the drive was taken to the rear wheels by two Coventry roller chains. The chains were adjusted by means of light cast-steel radius rods provided with screwed phosphor-bronze adjusting sleeves. The chassis price during the first three years was £1550. By 1924 there were two basic types, the S10 10-tonner at £1300 and the S12 12-tonner at £1400.

6A

6B

6C

6A: 'Exploded view' of chain final drive and brake mechanism.
6B: Showing the flexibility of the complete vehicle, circa 1921.
6C: Fine period picture of almost 16 tons of loaded Scammell 'Artic' belonging to Newberrys of Watford.
6D: Early application of a still-modern hydraulic tipping construction.

6D

7A-B: Many of the early solid-tyred Scammells were later converted to 'oilers' and/or fitted with 'pneumatics'. This one, built in 1921, had been modified almost beyond recognition when it was photographed again thirty years later.

7C-D: This Scammell tractor, registration No. YU 339, was converted by its owners (Pickfords; Fleet No. 914) in about 1936 and fitted with a Gardner diesel engine, pneumatic tyres, closed cab, and a hand-operated crane.

7C

7A

7B

7D

8A

8A: Scammell tractor with semi-trailer featuring oscillating axles, circa 1929. Note pneumatic-tyred front wheels.

8B: Showing the principle of oscillating axles. Both axles were mounted transversally on semi-elliptic leaf springs which in turn were attached to the frame on longitudinal pivots. The design was also known as 'four-wheels-in-line axles' and is still available as the 'Four trak'.

8C: Each trailer wheel had a simple mechanically operated brake with internally expanding shoes.

8B

8C

The first Scammells were conceived as load carriers and it is believed that the second vehicle, exported to the Gold Coast in 1921, is still operational. Other early specimens were later fitted with diesel engines and/or pneumatic tyres and saw active service for hundreds of thousands of miles. At the Olympia Motor Show in 1921 Scammell displayed a 27 × 7½ × 7 ft 'Pantechnicon' and a 2000-gal fuel oil tanker. The tank, built for Shell-Mex Ltd, had vertical sides and was rounded at the front end with the roof slightly cambered for extra strength. It rested on wooden bearers mounted rigidly on a drop-frame. At the back was a pumping set for loading and discharging the liquid, powered by a 2-cyl. 7-bhp Kelvin marine engine. This power unit, which was fitted with a reversing gear, operated an Albany gear pump via a Hardy flexible-disc joint. The vehicle's engine exhaust gases were piped through the tank to reduce the consistency of the oil. It was probably the first British 'articulated tanker'.

Tankers soon began to be a major item on Scammell's production programme and at times nearly 80% of the firm's home market sales comprised tractors with tanker semi-trailers. Not surprisingly, Scammells became known as experts on bulk-liquid transport problems. In 1929 they produced and patented their first frameless tanker and since then many thousands of frameless tankers of increasingly modernised specification have left the Scammell works for the carrying of liquids, powders and gases, as well as granular and flocculent solids.

9A

9B

9A: Two tanks on a drop-frame semi-trailer obviated weld failures which occurred in 'stepped' elliptical tanks with abrupt changes of section.
9B: 2000-gal 'D'-type twin-tank specially made by the Steel Barrel Co. Ltd of Uxbridge for use with the Scammell.
9C: 9-ton articulated frameless tanker with air compressor fitted to front of engine.
9D: Glass-lined frameless milk tank semi-trailer shown disconnected from the motive unit and resting on its 'landing gear'.

9C

9D

10A

10B

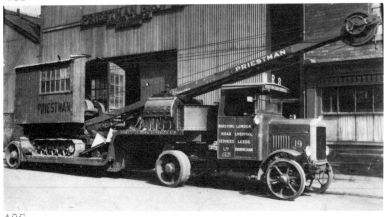

10C

10A-B-C, 11A-B-C: Some typical examples of heavy loads moved

Because the Scammell tractor and semi-trailer ('matched articulated vehicle') had proved so successful a separate company, Scammell Lorries Ltd, was formed with an authorised capital of £250,000. This was in July, 1922, and the six directors included Lt.-Col. Alfred George Scammell, his brother James Alan, and Mr Percy G. Hugh, an engineer. The registered offices were first at Holborn in London and later at Tolpits Lane, Watford, Herts., where in April, 1922, manufacturing premises had

11B

11C

...mmell tractive units with various types of semi-trailers.

11A

been taken over from G. Scammell and Nephew Ltd. The main plant and offices are still at the same location.

The original firm continued to operate at Spitalfields, under the direction of Mr H. R. Hood Barrs, and together with several other firms (including Anthony Hoists, Carrimore Six Wheelers, Midland Tipper Services, Steel Barrel Co.) became part of Steel Barrel Scammells and Associated Engineers Ltd. In 1965 the Spitalfields premises were sold.

12A: Chain-driven 'articulated eight-wheeler' with large balloon tyres for long-distance 'trunking'.
12B: Ten-ton drop-frame 'articulated six-wheeler' with loading crane.
12C: New low-loader outfit photographed in January, 1941. Note wartime 'blackout' features.
12D: Recent picture of well-preserved Scammell combination carrying Burrell Road Locomotive.
12E: Two wartime Scammells of Pickfords, a 4 × 2 and a 6 × 4 'Pioneer', on a moving job in 1952.
12F: The first frameless tanker of stepped elliptical construction was produced by Scammell in 1943.

12A

12D

12B

12E

12C

12F

13A

13D

13B

13E

13C

13F

13A: This 'Articulated Eight' was delivered in 1953.

13B: Gardner diesel-engined 'Highwayman' with 30-ton Scammell detachable axle drop-frame semi-trailer, 1960.

13C: A good deal of streamlining went into the body design of this 4330-US gal tanker, delivered to Cuba in 1953.

13D: This tractor of 1949 combined the characteristic Scammell radiator, separate headlamps and 'skirted' wings. From 1958 these tractors were named 'Highwayman'.

13E: The 'Handyman' Mk I appeared in 1960 and was of the 4 × 2 swb forward control design for use with maximum length semi-trailers.

13F: The 'Handyman' Mk III of 1964 featured a stylish glass-fibre cab, similar to that of the 8 × 2 'Routeman' Mk II.

14 A-B-C: Most impressive of them all? In 1929 Scammell introduced a very heavy tractor for use with semi-trailers for loads of up to 100 tons. Two were built. They had a 7-litre 80-bhp 4-cyl. petrol engine and an eight-speed gearbox. The maximum road speed was 5 to 6 mph and one gallon of fuel was consumed every mile. A jacking system was built in for elevating the load-carrying members and also for extracting the wheels should they break through the road surface. The first of these semi-trailers had a single row of rear wheels and was rated at 65 tons. At the end of its first journey, to Cornwall, it was left behind as a base for the stone crushing machine it was carrying!

14A

14B

14C

15A-B-C: Scammell 100-tonner Reg. No. KD 9168, after many years of hard work and the fitting of a diesel engine, was eventually acquired by Hardwicks of West Ewell, Surrey, who restored it to better-than-ever condition.

15D: The other 100-tonner was operated by Pickfords and had Reg. No. BLH 21, Fleet No. 1679. This tractive unit has also survived.
15E: Pickfords' vehicle, after change-over to diesel (note increased front overhang), pictured in Newcastle in 1937. Load: a 40,000 kw alternator stator, weighing $86\frac{3}{4}$ tons, destined for the City of Cape Town.

15A

15B

15C

15D

15E

16A-B-C-D: At the rear of the vehicle there was provision for steering the rear bogie which was often necessary to negotiate corners and sharp bends. There was telephonic communication between the driver of the motive unit and the rear steersman who was also responsible for signalling overtaking traffic and taking charge during reversing operations.

16A

16C

16B

16D

17A: Scammell 'Showtrac' tractors were specially built for Amusement Caterers and were equipped for towing trains of wagons and for generating electric current. Some had a winch as well.

17B: The Scammell 'Timber Tractor' was offered for forestry work. Shown is a 1928/29 model.

17C-D: This 45-ton drawbar tractor of the 1930s had a 85-bhp petrol engine, four speeds and chain drive. It is shown here hard at work in 1938 and during a rally at the Montagu Motor Museum after retirement in 1968.

17C

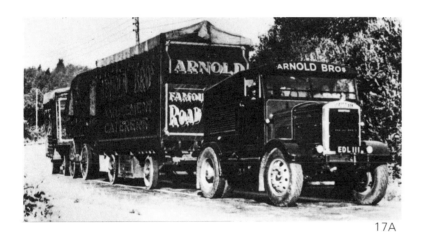

17A

17B

17D

'AUTO-VAN' AND AIR-COOLING

18A-B: The Scammell 'Auto-Van' was designed in about 1927/28 by Mr O. D. North, for local delivery work. The air-cooled 3-cyl. radial engine was mounted vertically over the gearbox/differential unit. The front brakes were 'inboard' and the front suspension independent with two transversal leaf springs. Load capacity was about 2 tons. Like an earlier O. D. North design, the North-Lucas car of 1923, the 'Auto-Van' suffered from engine cooling and induction problems and after one or two prototypes the project was shelved.

18C: Another interesting project was this rear-engined (Ford V8) independently-sprung car chassis of circa 1933/34. Only a scale model was built. Note striking similarity with certain Continental designs.
18D: In 1937 this 30-cwt platform truck was produced for the Great Western Railway. Suspension was by coil springs with hydraulic telescopic shock absorbers, and the air-cooled V-twin engine was integral with transmission and rear axle.

18A

18C

18B

18D

19A: Long-wheelbase chain-drive petrol-engined eight-tonner in the livery of Redburns of Enfield, circa 1930.
19B-C: Chain-drive eight-tonner fitted with 4-cyl. Dorman/Ricardo diesel engine and 'balloon' tyres. Circa 1932.

19A

19B

19C

6-TON 4×2 AND GARDNER DIESEL

20A-B: Six-tonner with pneumatic tyres and worm-drive rear axle, powered by six-cylinder Gardner 6LW diesel engine. This type of engine was widely used as standard equipment in various types of Scammells from 1933.

20C: The Six-ton 'Four-Wheeler' made its first appearance at the

Olympia Show in October 1928. It had the same 80-bhp engine as the 'Articulated Six-Wheeler' but featured a Kirkstall worm-drive rear axle and 40 × 8 pneumatic tyres. Wheelbase and body length were both 17 ft. The vehicle shown was delivered in 1932 and tows a Scammell-built full-trailer with 'Ackerman' steering.

20A

20C

20B

21A-B: Among the first Scammell Special vehicles were these 'Colonial' trucks, some of which were used in South America as early as 1928. Note the rear-mounted power winch with capstan pulley.

21C: Oilfields truck, 4 × 2, with midship winch mounting, very narrow cab, and 40 × 8 tyres.
21D: Early mobile (transit) concrete mixer.

21A

21C

21B

21D

22A-B-C: Shown here are some typical 'tropical proofed' Oilfield trucks
of the late 1940s and early 1950s. They were produced in three
wheelbase lengths (10 ft, 16 ft, 18 ft) and had Meadows 6-cyl. diesel
engines driving through Scammell six-speed gearboxes and Scammell
double reduction rear axles with spiral-bevel and epicyclic gearing.
Shown are a prototype tractor for semi-trailer and two flat-bed trucks,
one of which has a 'crew cab' and winch.

22A

22B

22C

23A: 'Rigid Six-Wheeler' with chain drive (6 × 2) of 1931–33. This was one of several operated by Wynns of Newport on their nightly London and South Wales trunk service during the 1930s.
23B: Typical early-thirties' cab with dash-mounted fuel tank.
23C: Interior of late-thirties' cab as fitted on 6 × 2 'Rigid Six'.
23D: Chassis of the 1933–39 6 × 2 model. These vehicles had a

Gardner 6LW diesel engine and an unconventional but successful Scammell rear bogie with bevel drive. Typical advanced features of this period were six-speed constant mesh gearboxes, double reduction epicyclic driving axles, rubber suspension and air brakes. The non-reactive rubber suspension rear bogie design was used on Scammell semi-trailers until 1969.

23A

23B

23C

23D

24A: Two special vehicles were produced in 1935 for the Anglo-Iranian Oil Co. Ltd for use in Iran (Persia). The 6 × 4 tractors had Parsons 160-bhp 8-cyl. petrol engines, 10-speed gearboxes and double reduction rear axles. Front suspension incorporated Gruss air springs. The tanks were made by Thompson Bros. of Bilston.

24B: Scammell 'Trunker' 6 × 4 tractor with four-wheel tank semi-trailer, 1960. Tractor had Gardner 6HLX diesel engine mounted behind 'Leylandish' cab. Only three of these were built.

24C: 'Trunker' Mk II 6 × 2 'twin-steer' 200-bhp (Gardner) motive unit with frameless tandem axle tank semi-trailer, 1965.

24D: Scammell's 6 × 4 for the 1970s is the 'Crusader', design and development of which started in 1967. Powered by a 290-bhp General Motors 8V-71 Series Detroit Diesel (or 272-bhp Leyland V8 801 Series), it is good for gross weights (GCW) of 44 tons and more.

24A

24B

24C

24D

25A-B-C-D: The year 1927 saw the introduction of this impressive 6 × 4 cross-country truck. As the illustrations show it featured a pivoted front axle and a single rear driving axle with rocking 'balancer' beams. These beams were in fact two oscillating gear cases with a driven wheel at each outer end. Any of the six wheels could rise to a height of 2 ft without twisting the frame. Shown here is the prototype vehicle which was used in many spectacular demonstrations. The name 'Pioneer' was applied later, probably because 'Rigid Six-Wheeler' sounded somewhat odd! When the 'Pioneer' was first conceived on the Scammell drawing boards in 1925/6 there were two versions: a 6 × 4 and a 6 × 6, both with independent front suspension with two transversally mounted leaf springs connecting the stub axle carriers. The rear suspension was designed and patented by Mr O. D. North, who was also responsible for many other Scammell innovations including the 100-tonner of 1929.

25A

25B

25C

25D

26A-B: The 'Pioneer' became very popular for 'colonial', oilfield and military use. Shown here is an early 'Colonial', with pipe-carrying body, fitted with overall chains round the rear wheels for maximum off-road performance.

26C: A 1928 'Pioneer' with 1200-gal tank and 800-gal tank trailer in operation in Perth, Western Australia.

26D: This 'Rigid Six-Wheeler' had a 'Pioneer' type rear bogie but conventional front suspension.

26A

26B

26C

26D

27A

27B

27A-B-C-D: 'Pioneer' oilfield chassis under test and being demonstrated with test body. Most 'Pioneers' from 1929 were fitted with the special pattern Still radiator which ensured the water level being above all the tubes should the vehicle be tilted. The large raised central water pot earned the 'Pioneer' the popular nickname 'Coffeepot Scammell'.

27C

27D

28A: This 'Pioneer' was specially fitted out for carrying pipes on oilfields. The narrow cab had a hinged roof for ease of entry and exit when long pipes were carried along the sides.
28B: Carrying 8 tons of pipes in Burmah (Burmah Shell Co.).

28C: View of the chassis, showing the rear-mounted 'light type' winch with its drive shaft and controls. Note also the gearbox-mounted tyre pump.

28A

28B

28C

29A-B: 'Pioneers' proved excellent off-road tree haulers. Semi-trailer bogie had rocking beams and single transversal leaf spring.

29C: Iraq Petroleum Co.'s 'Pioneer' pipe transporter off-loading with Scammell jib crane.

29D: Ancestor of the famous Scammell tank transporters, taking a loose gravel bank (gradient 1 in 2) with a test load of 17 tons.

29A

29C

29B

29D

'PIONEERS' AT WORK

30A: Watching a landslide being cleared, from the cab of a 'Coffeepot Scammell' in Brazil.
30B: Cargo carrier of South African Roadways, photographed in Durban, Natal.
30C: 'Pioneer' petrol tanker of the Anglo-Persian Oil Co. Ltd with specially reinforced chassis frame.

30A

30B

30C

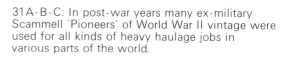

31A-B-C: In post-war years many ex-military Scammell 'Pioneers' of World War II vintage were used for all kinds of heavy haulage jobs in various parts of the world.

31A

31B

31C

32A

32B

32A-B: From 1928/29 the 'Pioneer' was also available with all-wheel drive and this is what it could do!
32C: A World War II 6 × 4 'Pioneer' heavy breakdown tractor was converted to a 6 × 6 in 1945/46 and became the prototype of the 'Explorer'.

32C

33A

33B

33C

33D

33E

33F

33A-B-C-D-E-F: After a considerable amount of development work, in 1933 Scammell introduced the 'Mechanical Horse' which later (1948) was developed into the 'Scarab'. Shown here are two of the prototypes, the 3-ton chassis, the engine, the steering/front suspension unit, the automatic coupling and the retractable 'landing gear'. It was designed to operate in turn with any number of semi-trailers. Since its inception over 20,000 have been delivered notably to railway companies all over the world. Similar vehicles were the Ford Tug, the Jen-Tug, the Karrier Cob and the Straussler Nippy. Scammell also marketed a 'Horse Shaft Attachment' which was interchangeable with the M.H. motive unit.

A logical development was the fitment of the Scammell instantaneous coupling gear to various approved makes of 4 × 2 tractor trucks. This enabled operators to use the three-wheeler for handling semi-trailers at terminals and in other congested areas, the four-wheelers taking over for longer journeys. The greater economy in handling by this method has resulted in the sale of some 100,000 of these semi-trailers for payloads of up to 12 tons in the past 30 years.

'MECHANICAL HORSES'

34A: Three-ton 'Mechanical Horse' with low-loader semi-trailer, 1935.
34B: Three-tonner with load-carrying bodywork and test load.
34C: Six-ton model operated in Lulea, Sweden, fitted with Swedish cab.
34D: French-built FAR 'Cheval Mécanique' outfits of the French Railways. These were built under Scammell licence by Chenard & Walcker, from 1938. There was also the smaller 'Pony Méchanique' (2-ton, 1940). Both had an air-cooled flat-twin engine.

34A

34B

34C

34D

35A

35B

35A: 'Scarab' 6-ton Mechanical Horse with Perkins P4 55-bhp diesel engine and 8-ton semi-trailer. Cape Town, 1960.
35B: 'Scarab' 3-tonner with 39-bhp petrol engine, 1960.
35C: 'Scarabs' on the assembly line. Engine, transmission and rear axle are built on the unit construction principle.
35D: 'Scarab-Four' 3—4-ton 4 × 2 motive unit with Standard cab, 1962.
35E: Among the last of the mechanical horses was this 'Townsman' 3-tonner, one of the large order placed by British Railways in 1964.

35D

35C

35E

36A-B-C-D: Scammell produced Gardner-engined 8 × 2 'Rigid Eight-Wheelers' with rubber rear suspension from 1935. Following the original models (an example of which is shown here, belonging to P & P Transport Co. of Bridgend) neither specification nor appearance changed much until the introduction of the 'Routeman' in 1960. A special sprocket-and-chain conversion kit was devised for emergency 'double-drive' use on icy roads.

36A

36C

36B

36D

37A: The 'Routeman' Mk I 8 × 2 was introduced in 1960 and was available with 150- or 161-bhp diesel engine (Gardner or Leyland), and manual or power-assisted steering. A few 'Routeman' chassis were built with 6 × 2 and 8 × 4 drive.

37B: The 'Routeman' Mk II made its appearance in 1962 and featured a Michelotti-designed glass-fibre cab. Shown is a 1964 8 × 2 with Bonallack 'Pneumajector' tank for bulk transport of cement with low-pressure pneumatic discharge. The Mk III was an 8 × 4, plated at 26 tons GVW.

37C: Special 8 × 6 Motorway Gritting Machine and Snowplough, one of seven built in 1960 for Ministry of Transport. 12-speed transmission.

37D: Scammell's latest: 'Samson' 8 × 4 motive unit for 75 tons GCW. Fifth wheel load 27 tons. Introduced at 1970 Commercial Motor Show, powered by a 290-bhp General Motors V8 diesel engine (8V71N).

37A

37C

37B

37D

THE 'CONTRACTOR'

38A-B: In 1964 the 'Contractor' was introduced, as a new 6 × 4 tractor for semi-trailers or drawbar tractor for full-trailers. It has been offered with various diesel engines including AEC, Cummins and Rolls-Royce, and gearboxes varying from 7-speed manual to 10-speed semi-automatic. Gross combination weight (GCW) is 75 tons. Shown here are some of these tractors as operated in Britain (Wynns), and South Africa (S.A.U.M.).

38A

38B

39A

39B

39A: Interior view of the cockpit of a 'Contractor' with semi-automatic transmission.

39B: Mr John Wynn, director of the Robert Wynn & Sons Ltd in Newport, Wales, with one of the 'Contractors' which replace their well-known fleet of much-modified ex-US Army Pacific M26 tractors, one of which is shown alongside.

39C: Scammell 'Contractor', one of several converted into an 8 × 4 truck/tractor in Western Australia. This 'road train' is used in iron ore country in the far north-west of Western Australia.

39C

The 'Constructor' was a six-wheel drive heavy duty vehicle designed specifically for operating under the arduous off-road conditions found in oilfields, hydro-electric schemes, civil engineering construction sites and the like. This model was first introduced in 1952 and in 1956 also became available as a 6×4 ('Junior Constructor'). Various makes of diesel power units were available, including Rolls-Royce and Cummins, up to 200 bhp.

40A: Long-wheelbase truck/tractor for oilfield work in Australia.
40B: The 'Constructor' chassis as base for a mobile revolving crane.
40C: Wrecking truck fitted out by Harpers of Guildford for oilfield use by Shell in British Borneo, 1955 (Shell photograph).

40A

40B

40C

41A

41A: A pair of 'Constructors' with a multi-wheeled low-bed transporter between them.
41B: When negotiating a tight corner during a test by *Commercial Motor* on a 'Constructor' with Crane 45–65-ton eight-wheeler trailer, it was found easier to drive the vehicle up this bank than to shunt backwards and forwards.
41C: A 'Constructor' for oilfield use under construction at the Scammell works in Watford. Note sturdy bumper/radiator guard.

41B by kind permission of *Commercial Motor*

41C

42A-B-C-D-E: Some typical applications of the 'Constructor' for oilfield work, including 'bed trucks' and drilling outfits.

One of the vehicles shown, 42E, is fitted with special equipment for oil-well services. It is used for pumping liquid cement for pipe casing, acid into limestone rock, fracturing fluids into sandstone etc. The two pumps, driven by 320-bhp GM diesel engines, can handle any fluid from liquid nitrogen to heavy muds at 20 lb/gal and at pressures up to 12,000 lb/sq in.

42A

42B

42C

42D

42E

43A-B-C: The 'Super Constructor' 6 × 6, introduced in 1958, was available with various engines including a Leyland/Albion 15.2-litre 237-bhp diesel and a Rolls-Royce supercharged 12.17-litre unit developing 250 bhp. The transmission consisted of a fluid coupling with semi-automatic eight-speed gearbox and a single-speed transfer box. Shown are two draw-bar tractor versions and a tractor with Crane semi-trailer and front-mounted crane jib.

43B

43A

43C

THE 'MOUNTAINEER'

44A-B-C-D: The 'Mountaineer' was first produced in 1949 and could be called the 4 × 4 version of the 6 × 6 'Constructor' (or vice versa). Its uses were varied and shown here are some heavy 8/10-cu yd dump trucks and two 60-ton GTW drawbar tractors. Various power units were available including Leyland (150 bhp), Gardner (112 and 150 bhp) and Rolls-Royce (150 bhp).

44A

44B

44C

44D

45A: The 'Mountaineer' as a load carrier. Like other Scammell cross-country vehicles the front axle is mounted on a pivoted transversal leaf spring for maximum articulation.
45B: Wrecking truck with winch and ground anchor, fitted out by Reynolds Boughton of Amersham.
45C: Oilfield truck in very loose desert sand. The cab roof shield provides protection from direct sun.

45A

45B

45C

'MOUNTAINEERS' WITH SEMI-TRAILERS

46A-B-C-D: The 'Mountaineer' as a tractor with 'fifth wheel' for semi-trailers. The flat platform semi-trailer shown has a load capacity of 56,000 lb. 'Mountaineers' are also used for the mounting of tank bodies, transit cement mixers etc. The bus semi-trailer, 46D, is a Scammell/Crane 126-seater, with Sparshatts/Rollalong bodywork of 1962.

46A

46B

46C

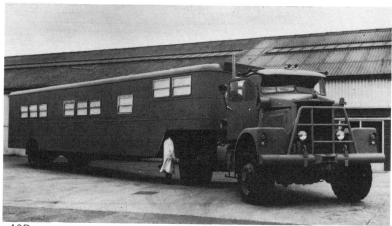

46D

Special dump truck chassis were the 4×2 'Sherpa' and the 6×4 'Himalayan', introduced in 1959 and 1961 respectively.

47A: 20-ton GVW 8/10-cu yd 'Sherpa', designed to operate on or off the public highway. A 9/11-cu yd version with 22½-ton GVW was available for off-road use only.

47B: 30½-ton GVW 12/14-cu yd 'Himalayan'. Both 'Sherpa' and 'Himalayan' had Leyland 'Power Plus' P.680 diesel engines. There was also a road tractor version of the 'Himalayan' with full-width cab.

47A

47B

Ever since the advent of the 6×4 'Pioneer' in
1926/27 the military have looked to Scammells for
heavy duty cross-country vehicles and many
Scammells were produced as a direct result of a
specific military requirement. During 1939–42
some special forward control tractors were
designed, including a 200-bhp model with
detachable oscillating half-axle rear bogie (four
driven wheels in line), a 6×6 unit with engine
behind cab, and an 8×8 with two Gardner diesels
and all-wheel steering. Actual production,
however, did not follow. Illustrated here are some
rare military Scammells with fewer than six wheels.

48A: The 6-ton 'Mechanical Horse' in Royal
Navy livery. Note soft-top cab and ballast box.
Used as drawbar tractor.
48B: 'Mechanical Horse' with semi-trailer
specially designed for transport of military
Airspeed 'Oxford' aircraft. In 1937 a towing
attachment was designed for coupling the 6-in.
Howitzer and 60-pdr Mk III and IV Field Guns
to the 'Mechanical Horse'.
48C: Four-wheel drive drawbar/winch tractor
produced for the Royal Navy in 1939.

48B

48A

48C

During the late 1930s Scammells produced gun tractors, using the versatile 'Pioneer' chassis. Manufacture of these vehicles continued until 1944 after some detail modifications had been introduced in 1938, including the fitting of a vertical instead of a horizontal winch. Total production was 786 units (1939-1944).

49A: Bird's eye view of the 'Pioneer' chassis with horizontal winch, 1937.
49B: Early Gun Tractor, showing machine-gun mounting in roof of crew compartment. Note tyre chains in the side lockers.
49C: Loading shells by means of pulley block.
49D: There was a special technique for cranking the Gardner diesel engine of the 'Coffeepot Scammells'. (Heavy B/D Tractor shown)

49A

49C

49B

49D

SCAMMELL 'BREAKDOWNS'

The best-known wartime Scammell was undoubtedly the 'Pioneer' Heavy Breakdown Recovery tractor. Many of these remained in use after the war either in military service or by civilian operators. Some are still operational today. The actual production period was 1939–1946, during which nearly 1500 were supplied.

50A: Three-quarter rear view of the Model SV/2S which had a Herbert Morris sliding-jib 2½-ton crane. SV/1T and 1S had collapsible jibs but were rare.
50B: One attempt to modernise the Scammell's appearance by Stormonts of Tunbridge Wells, Kent.
50C: Most Scammell 'Breakdowns' were only little modified for civilian use. Note detachable ballast weights at front end.
50D: 'Breakdown' with fixed front wings and soft-top cab (Dutch Army modifications).
50E: This much-modified recovery vehicle is operated by Caffyns of Canterbury, Kent. The extensive conversion was made in 1965.

50A

50B

50D

50C

50E

51A

51B

51A-B: Early 'Pioneer' 6 × 4–4 tank transporting unit. The tank carried is a 'Medium' Mk II. Note that semi-trailer rear bogie is detachable for loading and unloading operations.

51C: Motive unit of 20-ton tank transporter with test load. Note 'undersize' front tyres (10.50 × 20 vs. 15.00 × 20 rear) which were a feature of this early model. A total of 548 tank transporters were delivered to the Army during 1939–45.

51D: Post-war military conversion of 30-ton motive unit: drawbar tractor with concrete ballast weights.

51C

51D

52A: Transporter, 20-ton, 6 × 4—8, Recovery. This model had horizontal 'runways'. The cab seated three in front, four in the rear compartment. A Scammell 8-ton vertical spindle type winch was fitted.

52B: A 30-ton tank transporter carrying a 'Sherman' M4 medium tank in the North African desert, followed by a topless AEC 'Matador' and a variety of other 'soft-skin' ('B') vehicles.

52C: The design of the 'Pioneer' rear bogie made conversion to the half-track configuration a feasible operation.

52D-E-F: The haulage of tanks on semi- and full-trailers is not always an operation carried out by the military themselves, as these Pickfords photos show.

52A

52B

52C

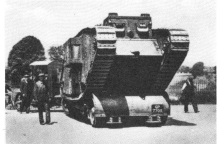

52D

52E

52F

53A: In 1928/29 the first military 'Pioneer' 6 × 6 appeared. Note the hefty front axle.

53B: Fitted with a test body and towing a trailer, the 6 × 6 is shown here during a military demonstration near Aldershot. Following is an 8 × 8 Guy.

53C: Production model of the 'Pioneer' 6 × 6 Gun Tractor (Indian Army)

53D-E-F-G: Details of the winch and the arrangement for use at either the rear or front of the vehicle.

53A

53B

53C

53D

53F

53E

53G

54A: Shortly after the War the 6 × 6 'Explorer' was developed (from the 'Pioneer') and from about 1950 large numbers were supplied with Breakdown/Recovery equipment for military use. Engine was a Meadows 10.35-litre 175-bhp 6-cyl. petrol unit.

54B: 'Explorer' recovery vehicle as supplied to the New Zealand Army in 1959. These vehicles had the optional Meadows 6DC630 diesel engine.

54C: The general layout, the suspension and details such as the means by which the winch cable can be used for pulling at the front of the vehicle are basically the same as on the 'Pioneer' of 1928/29.

54D: REME 'Breakdown' unloading a 1914 military horse-drawn GS Wagon at the Army School of Transport Museum, Bordon, Hants (1969). Note fully extended jib.

54A

54C

54B

54D

55A-B-C-D-E-F: The 6 × 6 'Constructor' proved very suitable for several types of military applications including Rolls-Royce-engined tractors for high-capacity full- and semi-trailers. As can be seen, various types of cabs, wings, bumpers and equipment have been used over the years (1952/3 onwards).

55A

55D

55B

55E

55C

55F

56A-B-C: About 1928/29 design and development work was carried out on some armoured car projects. Shown here is a scale model of an interesting type based on the 'Pioneer' design but fitted with a radial type engine at the rear and independent front suspension at the ends of a centrally pivoted axle (patented by Scammell Lorries Ltd and Messrs O. D. North and P. G. Hugh). A full-size model was not produced.

56A

56B

56C

57A-B-C-D-E-F: The Scammell armoured car that did get beyond the drawing-board stage, early in 1929. It had a special drop frame chassis, derived from the 'Pioneer', in order to achieve a low silhouette. The bodywork of the 'completed' vehicle shown was in fact a mock-up, made largely of wood. The vehicle was to have had two revolving turrets but the project was shelved.

57A

57D

57B

57C

57E

57F

The 'Mechanical Horse' and the 'Scarab' were widely used for municipal work, both at home and abroad. An extensive range of bodies, trailers and equipment was offered.

58A: Common 'Dustcart', 3 × 2; this one was acquired by the City of Leeds in 1936.
58B: The very tight turning circle of this 1933 'Mechanical Horse' with large-capacity refuse collector semi-trailer, made the real horse-drawn outfit in the background look rather antiquated.

58C: This poison gas decontaminator was a Scammell wartime development.
58D: Post-war 'Scarab' sprinkler/road sweeper working in the market square of Helsinki, Finland. Russian church in background.

58A

58C

58B

58D

59A-B-C: It is not generally known that Scammell built fire engines and other fire-fighting equipment. Shown here and on the following page are two types of fire appliances of the Watford Fire Brigade (mid-1930s).

59A

59C

59B

60A-B: Scammell fire tender of the Borough of Watford, Scammell's home town, supplied in 1935.

60A

60B

61A-B: During the early part of the second World War Scammell produced large numbers of fire pumps of the portable, towable (trailer) and wheelbarrow type.

61C: Built in 1938 as an AFS (Auxiliary Fire Service) appliance with trailer pump, this equipment was used until 1969 as a works' fire engine.

61D: A modern 6 × 6 'Constructor' fire-fighting appliance for oil-well service. The discharge capacity of this unit is not less than 1800 gal of foam per minute. Supplied to the Halliburton Drilling Co.

61A

61B

61C

61D

In addition to complete 'articulated vehicles', Scammells have over the years also supplied thousands of semi-trailers for use in conjunction with tractive units of other makes, notably Bedford. Some examples are shown here. A special trailer factory was set up in 1940 at Moor Park, not far from the main plant, and extended in 1941. A Scammell development of the mid-1960s was a heavy-duty fully automatic coupling for their maximum-capacity articulated vehicles. An instantaneous telescopic-leg type, it was particularly suitable for semi-trailers which are often parked as temporary storage containers or left at depots by long-distance hauliers for simple and speedy change-over from one tractive unit to another. Keeping pace with demands for the bulk transport of materials in powder, liquid and gaseous forms, the company has produced semi-trailers designed for these, the loads being air-conditioned, frozen or heated electrically while on the move. Gases and liquified gases are catered for by special pressure containers and frameless tankers capable of conveying loads at pressures of up to 3,000 lb/sq in. and at sub-temperatures down to minus 183°C. These tankers have linings of rubber, glass, Lithcote etc.

Other products include full drop frame transporter trailers suitable for heavy individual loads. Rubber, air and conventional steel spring suspension designs are used for these and other Scammell trailers.

62A

62B

62C

62A: Military Bedford OXC tractor with GS type semi-trailer, one of many different types supplied to the Services during World War II.
62B: Dennis tractive unit with refuse-collecting semi-trailer.
62C: Bedford OSS/Scammell flat-bed outfit, carrying Campbell's 2400-bhp Rolls-Royce-engined motor boat 'Bluebird', 1949.
62D: Royal Navy tanker semi-trailer with automatic coupling/landing gear.

62D

63A

63B

63C

63D

In 1955 Scammell became part of British Leyland. This brought about a good many changes but Scammell did not lose its identity. It is also interesting to observe that because they are not mass-producers of motor vehicles the whole atmosphere at a factory like Scammell is different from that at most other vehicle-manufacturing plants. This is reflected in a different kind of relationship between the company and its employees, many of whom have spent all their working lives there. Mr Walter F. Hall, a retired executive, put it like this: 'During my many years with Scammell, the interest of the staff in their jobs was vocational. We specialised in specials and variety conditioned our lives'. Mr Hall, after serving an indentured apprenticeship with the parent firm of G. Scammell and Nephew Ltd, was transferred to Scammell Lorries Ltd where he held various posts until he retired as manager of the Special Products division in 1968.

Another example of a 'life-long' career with Scammell was Mr Francis E. Chesney who retired in 1961 after 42 years' unbroken service. He was the company's senior transport officer and the way in which he came to join is of particular interest. At the age of sixteen he was passionately fond of horses and as a means of riding and working with them he joined the 5th London Brigade of the Royal Field Artillery, Territorial Army. The commanding officer happened to be a Major Scammell. When war broke out in 1914, the Brigade went to France and Mr Chesney served with them through all the major campaigns, including the Battle of the Somme. After demobilisation in 1919 he was unemployed for a time, in common with many ex-service men, until he remembered that his C.O. had a business in which he might find employment as a driver – and so began his career. At that time the (original) company was manufacturing horse carts but he soon got involved in the first powered Scammell 'Artics'. By the time of his retirement he had covered over one-and-a-half million miles (with a 'clean' licence) in almost everything from cars to the heaviest of the Scammell 'heavies'.

63A: Bedford/Scammell with modernised wings, towing Prestcold Refrigeration Mobile Exhibition unit of Pressed Steel Co. Ltd. One of four, built in 1949.
63B: Bedford TA Series tractor with Scammell dropside platform semi-trailer.
63C: Bedford/Scammell collecting a loaded semi-trailer from the London docks after having returned an empty unit, circa 1947.
63D: Bedford Model SAO, 1955, petrol tanker. Powered by Perkins R6 diesel engine.

INDEX

NOTE: types are indicated by wheel configuration, e.g. 3×2 is a vehicle with three wheels, two of which are driven. 6×6–8 indicates a six-wheel drive tractive unit with eight-wheel semi-trailer. Dual tyres count as one wheel.